# John Denver
## FOLK SINGER

## Contents

Cover Photo: Francois Lehr/SIPA Press

Transcribed by Jeff Jacobson
Additional transcribing by Peter Seckel and Kenn Chipkin

Cherry Lane Music Company
Director of Publications/Project Editor: Mark Phillips
Manager of Publications: Gabrielle Fastman

ISBN-13: 978-1-57560-942-3
ISBN-10: 1-57560-942-8

*Visit our website at www.cherrylane.com*

# DARCY FARROW

Words and Music by
Steve Gillette and Tom Campbell

Drop D tuning, capo 3rd fret:
(low to high) D-A-D-G-B-E

**Intro**
**Moderately, in 2**

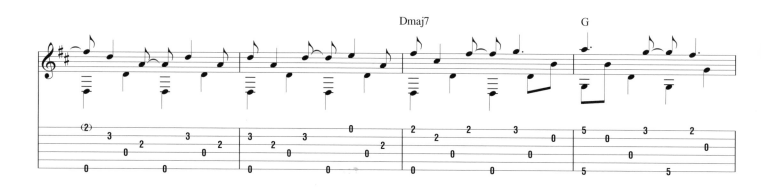

*All music sounds a minor 3rd higher than written. Capoed fret is "0" in tab.

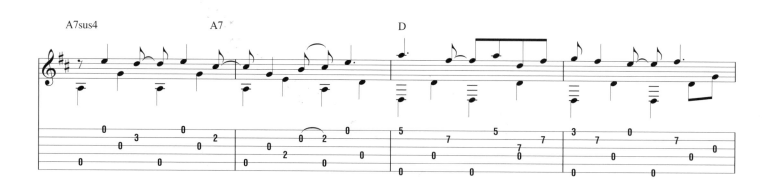

D G D A D
1. Where the Walk -
Verse
D G
- er runs down to the Car - son Val - ley Plain,
was as sweet as the sug - ar can - dy;
- ny did stum - ble and she did fall;
D
there lived a maid -
her touch was as soft
her dy - in' touched the hearts
Dmaj7 Em7 A7
- en; Dar - cy Far - row was her name.
as a bed of goose down.
of us, one and all.

She prom - ised ___ to wed ___ be - fore ___ the snows ___
and to young Van - dy, whose

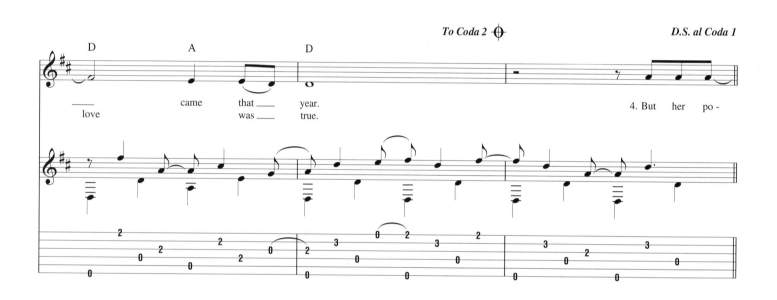

*To Coda 2* ⊕      *D.S. al Coda 1*

love came that ___ year.
was ___ true.

4. But her po -

⊕ **Coda 1**

**Interlude**

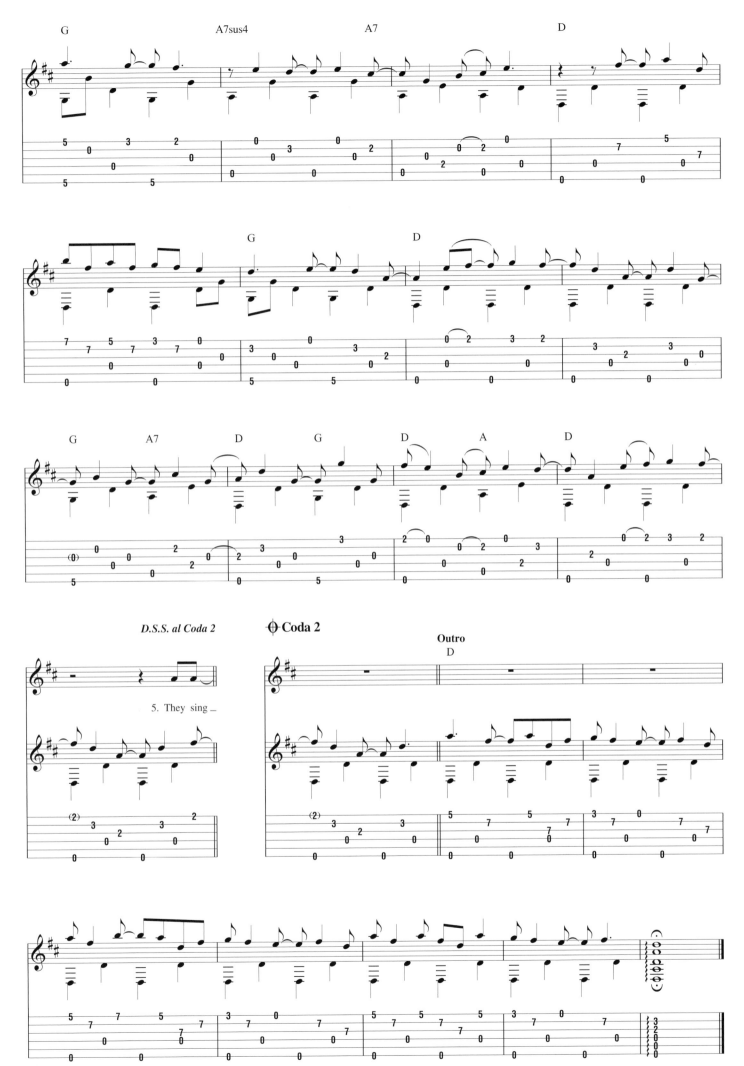

# FLY AWAY

Words and Music by
John Denver

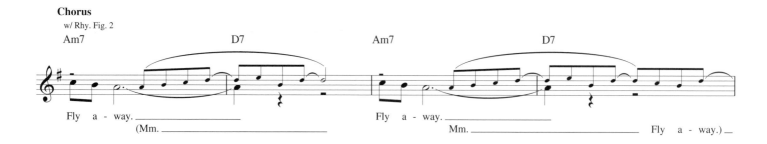

**Chorus**
w/ Rhy. Fig. 2

Am7          D7          Am7          D7

Fly a - way.          Fly a - way.
(Mm.          Mm.          Fly a - way.)

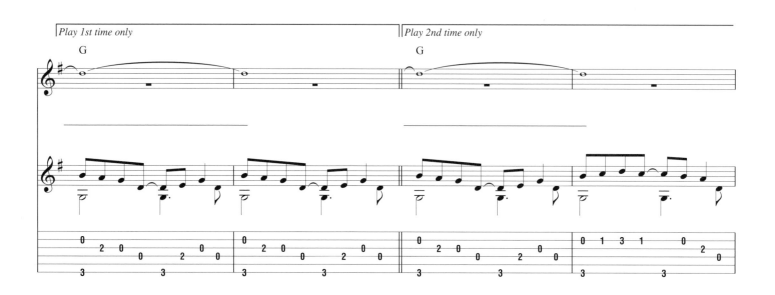

*Play 1st time only*          *Play 2nd time only*

G          G

**Bridge**
Am

In this whole world there's no - bod -

Bm          C

- y as lone - ly as she.          There's

11

# GARDEN SONG

Words and Music by
Dave Mallett

Drop D tuning, capo 2nd fret:
(low to high) D-A-D-G-B-E

**Intro**
**Moderately, in 2**

Acous. gtr.

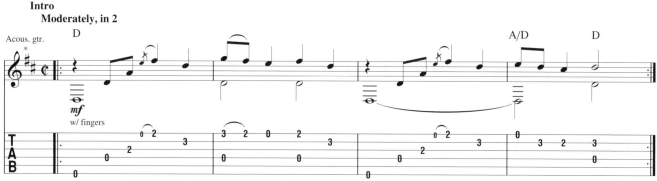

*All music sounds a whole step higher than written. Capoed fret is "0" in tab.

**Verse**

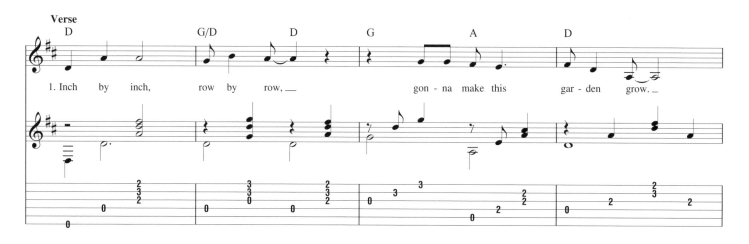

1. Inch by inch, row by row, __ gon-na make this gar-den grow. __

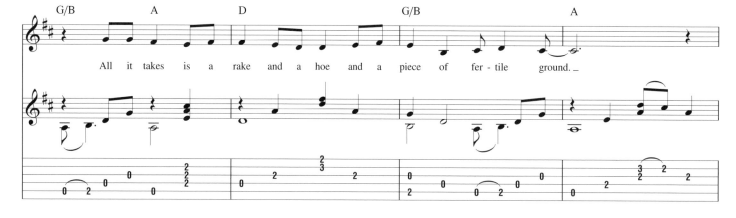

All it takes is a rake and a hoe and a piece of fer-tile ground. __

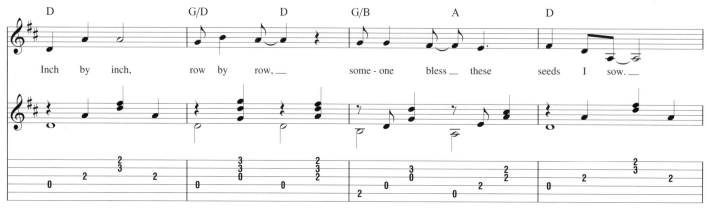

Inch by inch, row by row, __ some-one bless __ these seeds I sow. __

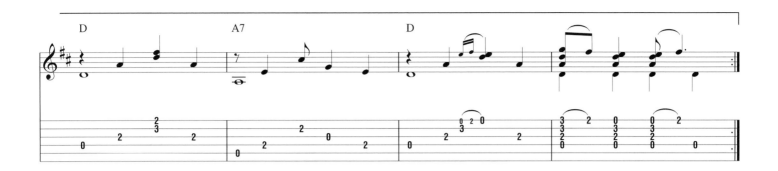

*D.S. al Coda*

**Coda**

**Outro**

rain    comes    tum - bl - ing    down.

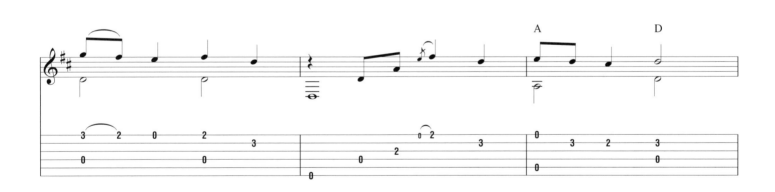

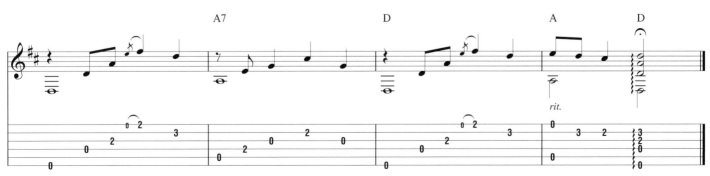

*rit.*

# LEAVING ON A JET PLANE

Words and Music by
John Denver

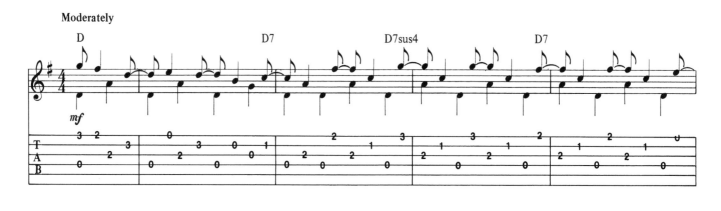

Moderately

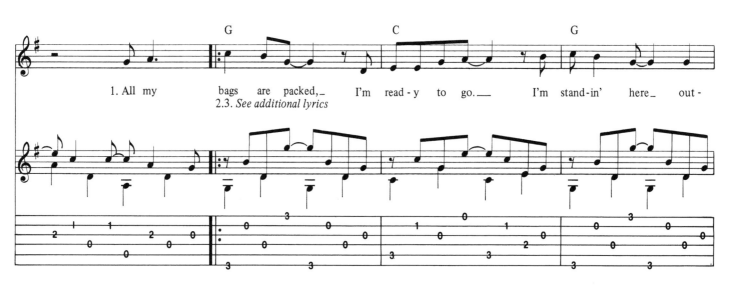

1. All my bags are packed,__ I'm read-y to go.__ I'm stand-in' here__ out-
2.3. *See additional lyrics*

side your door.__ I hate to wake you up to say good-bye.

### Additional Lyrics

2. There's so many times I've let you down,
   So many times I've played around,
   I tell you now they don't mean a thing.
   Every place I go I'll think of you,
   Every song I sing I'll sing for you,
   When I come back I'll bring your wedding ring.

   *Chorus*

3. Now the time has come to leave you,
   One more time let me kiss you,
   Then close your eyes, I'll be on my way.
   Dream about the days to come,
   When I won't have to leave alone,
   About the times I won't have to say:

   *Chorus*

# MOTHER NATURE'S SON

Words and Music by
John Lennon and Paul McCartney

Drop D tuning, capo 2nd fret:
(low to high) D-A-D-G-B-E

**Intro**
**Moderately**

**Play downstemmed notes w/ thumb; strum upstemmed notes w/ fingers.
*All music sounds a whole step higher than written. Capoed fret is "0" in tab.

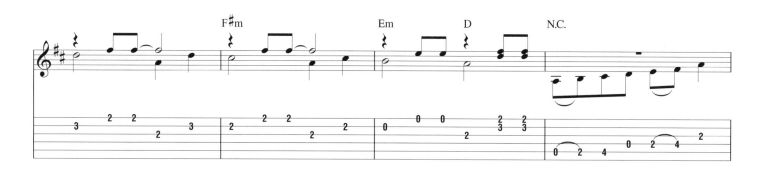

***T = Thumb on 6th string

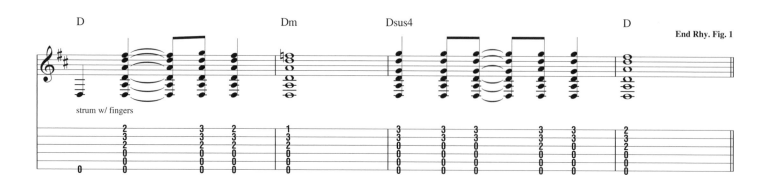

**§ Verse**

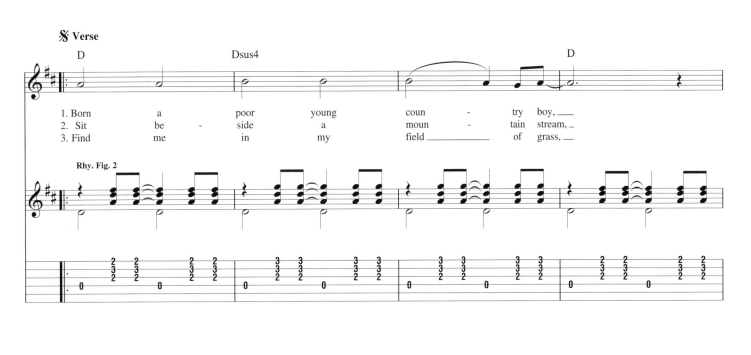

1. Born a poor young coun - try boy,
2. Sit be - side a moun - tain stream,
3. Find me in my field of grass,

**Rhy. Fig. 2**

Moth - er Na - ture's son.
watch her wa - ters rise.
Moth - er na - ture's son.

**End Rhy. Fig. 2**

**w/ Rhy. Fig. 1**

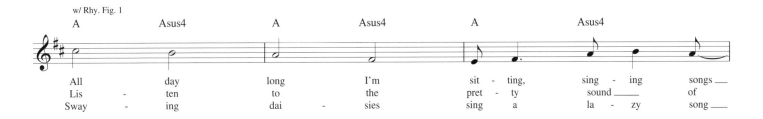

All day long I'm sit - ting, sing - ing songs for ev - 'ry - one.
Lis - ten to the pret - ty sound of mu - sic as she flies.
Sway - ing dai - sies sing a la - zy song be - neath the sun.

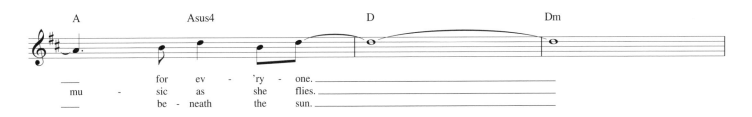

**To Coda ⊕** | 1. | 2.

Du du

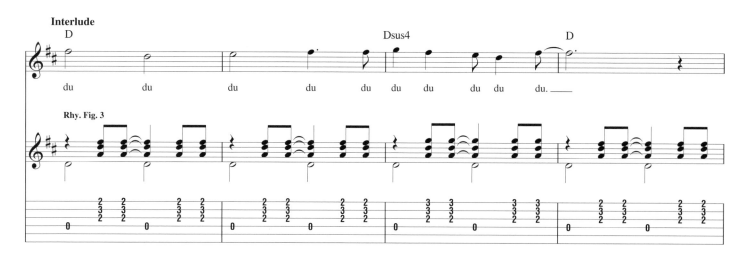

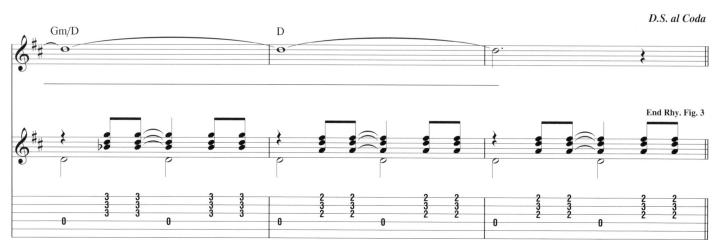

# MR. BOJANGLES

Words and Music by
Jerry Jeff Walker

Capo III

**Intro**
**Bright Waltz**

*All music sounds a minor 3rd higher than indicated. Capoed fret is "0" in tab.

𝄋 **Verse**

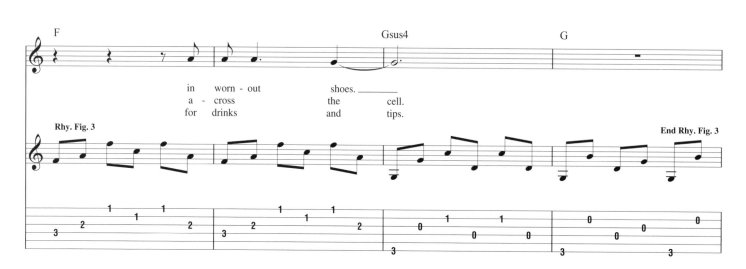

|     | knew | a | man | Bo | - | jan | - | gles | and | he | danced | for | you |
| --- | said | the | name | Bo | - | jan | - | gles | and | he | danced | a | lick |
|     | said, | "I | dance | now | at | ev | - | 'ry | chance | in | hon | - | ky - tonks |

| in | worn - out | shoes. |
| a - | cross | the | cell. |
| for | drinks | and | tips. |

# PARADISE

Words and Music by
John Prine

**Intro**
**Moderately slow, in 1**

1. When

**Verse**

I was a child, _____ my fam - 'ly would _____
some - times we'd trav - el _____ right down _____ the Green _____
coal com - p'ny came _____ with the world's _____ larg - est _____

trav - el down to west - ern Ken - tuck - y where my
Riv - er to the a - ban - doned old pris - on where down
shov - el, and they tor - tured the tim - ber and

# POTTER'S WHEEL

Words and Music by
Bill Danoff

Drop D tuning:
(low to high) D-A-D-G-B-E

**Intro**
**Moderately slow, in 2**

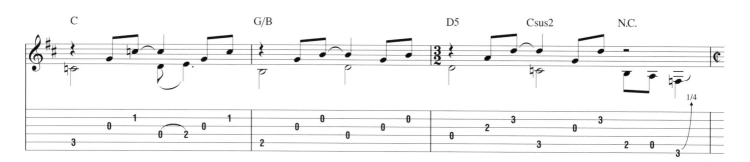

**𝄋 Verse**

fast _____ be - com - ing _____ young - er; the news is
life _____ the blood - y _____ sto - ry, teach to their
chil - dren will be _____ dig - ging in some

**Rhy. Fig. 1**

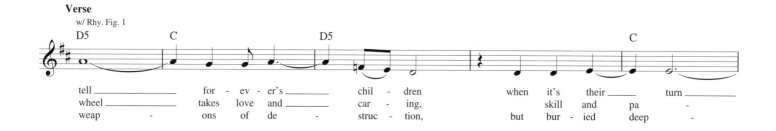

**Verse**

w/ Rhy. Fig. 1

tell _____ for - ev - er's _____ chil - dren    when it's their _____ turn _____
wheel _____ takes love and _____ car - ing,    skill and pa -
weap - ons of de - struc - tion,    but bur - ied deep

_____ to hurt and _____ heal? _____    What - ev - er spins _____
- tience fast and _____ slow.    The works it makes _____
- er in the _____ hole _____    they'll find a mes -

_____ a grim tor - na - do    can al - so turn _____ a pot - ter's
_____ are eas - 'ly _____ bro - ken    once they sur - vive _____ the pot - ter's
- sage and \_\_ a _____ prom - ise    in the sand, _____ the pot - ter's

**Chorus**

wheel.
throw.
bowl.

Take a lit - tle clay,    put it on the wheel,

Rhy. Fig. 2

get a lit - tle hint how God must feel.

End Rhy. Fig. 2

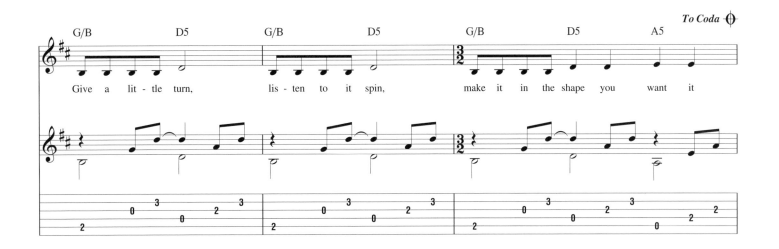

Give a lit-tle turn, lis-ten to it spin, make it in the shape you want it

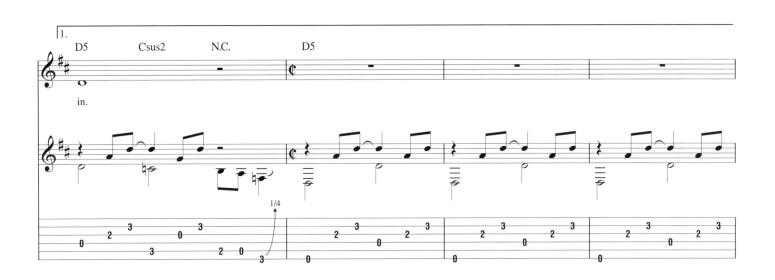

1.

in.

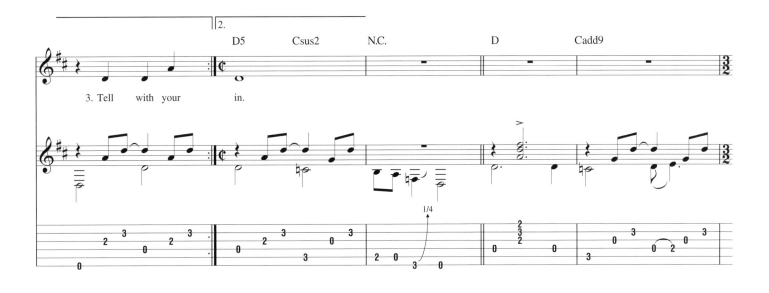

2.

3. Tell with your in.

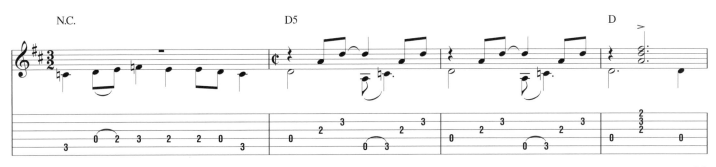

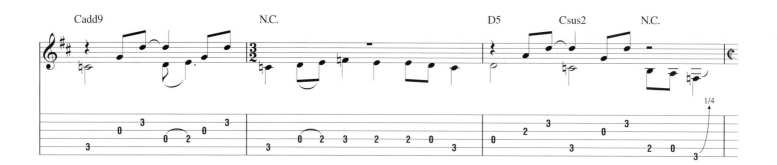

**D.S. al Coda**

5. Some - day some

**⊕ Coda**

w/ Rhy. Fig. 2 (last 2 meas.)      w/ Rhy. Fig. 2 (2 times)

in.                     Take a lit - tle clay,      put it on the wheel,

get a lit - tle hint how God must __ feel.                Give a lit - tle turn,

lis - ten to it spin,      make it in the shape you want it ___ in.

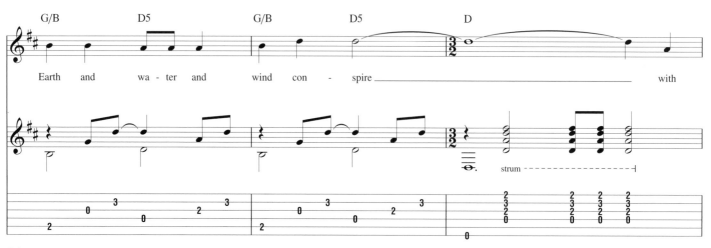

Earth and wa - ter and wind con - spire _____ with

strum - - - - - - - - - - - - - -

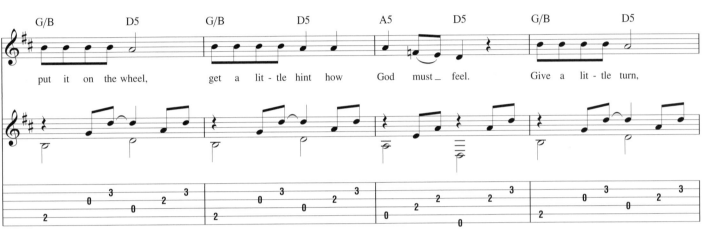

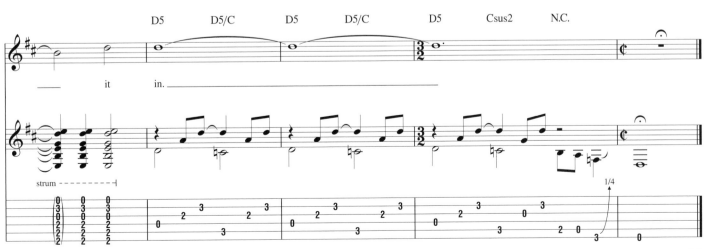

# I GUESS HE'D RATHER
# BE IN COLORADO

Words and Music by
Bill Danoff and Taffy Nivert Danoff

*T = Thumb on 6th string

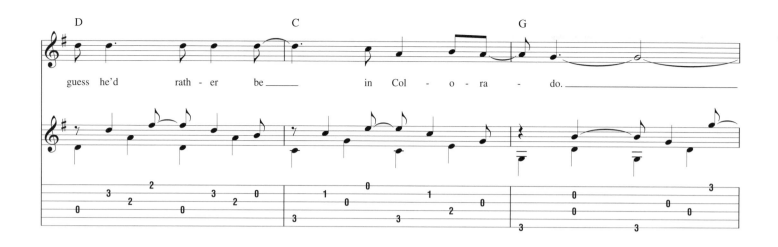

guess he'd rath - er be _____ in Col - o - ra - do. _____

Interlude

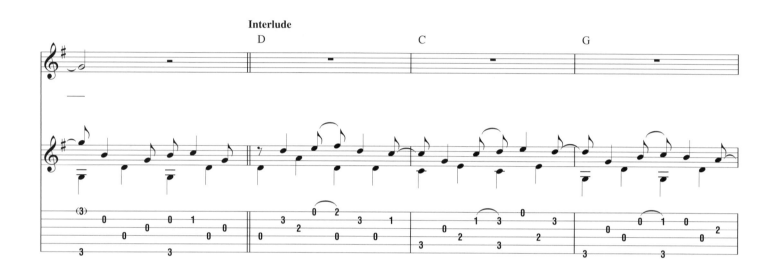

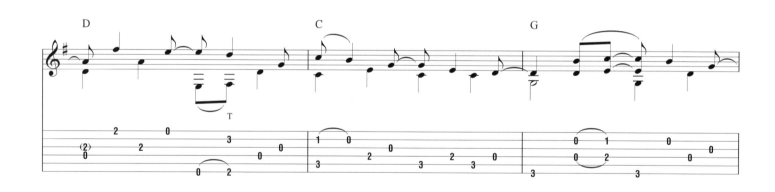

*D.S. al Coda*

3. I

𝄌 **Coda**

- y. _____

# RHYMES AND REASON

Words and Music by
John Denver

*John Denver often played this song tuned down a half or whole step.

**T = Thumb on 6th string

Lyrics:
1. So you speak ___ to me ___ of sad - ness, the com - ing of ___ the win - ter, ___ The
cit - ies start ___ to crum - ble and the tow - ers fall ___ a - round ___ us. ___ The

39

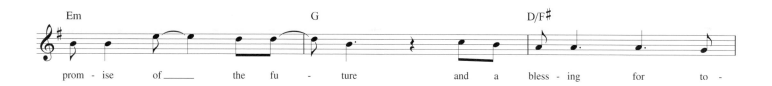

prom - ise of _____ the fu - ture and a bless - ing for to -

day. _____

*D.S. al Coda*

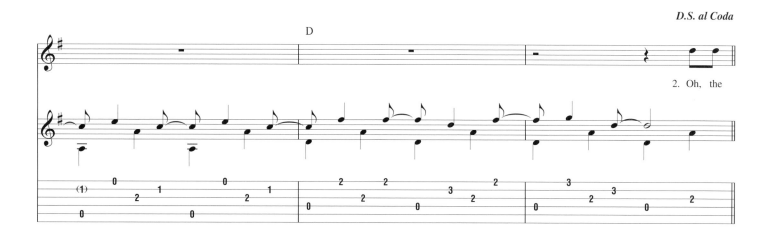

2. Oh, the

**⊕ Coda**

_____ us to be free. _____ For the

**Chorus**
w/ Rhy. Fig. 1 (1st 8 meas.)

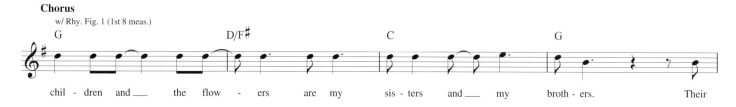

chil - dren and _____ the flow - ers are my sis - ters and _____ my broth - ers. Their

laugh-ter and ___ their love - li - ness ___ would clear a cloud-y day. ___ And the song ___

___ that I am sing - ing ___ is a prayer to non - be - liev - ers. ___

Come and stand be - side us; we can find a bet - ter way. ___

**Outro**

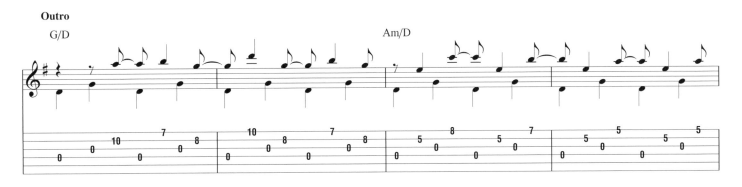

*rit.*

43

# ROCKY MOUNTAIN HIGH

Words and Music by
John Denver and Mike Taylor

Tune down:
⑥ = D

Moderately slow, in 2

(Strum chords shown in TAB)

1. He was born

in the sum-mer of his twen-ty-sev-enth year,     com-in'

2.-5. See additional lyrics

sim.

*To play along with recording, place capo at 2nd fret.

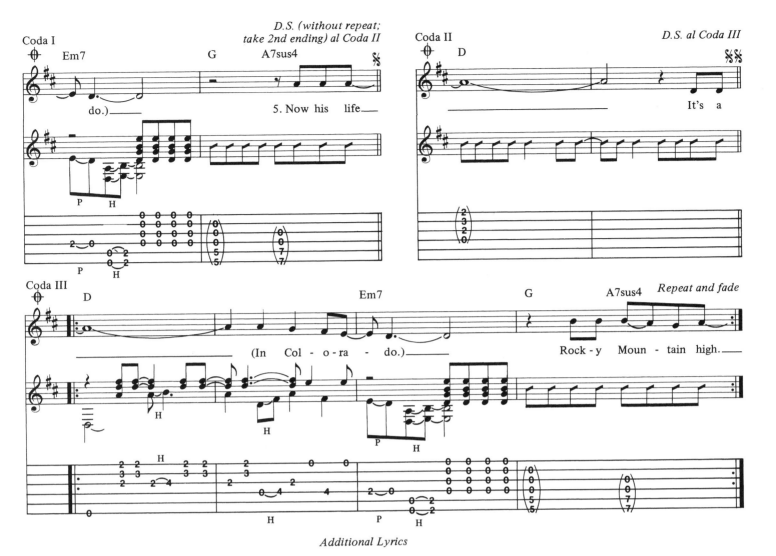

*Additional Lyrics*

2. When he first came to the mountains his life was far away,
   On the road and hangin' by a song.
   But the string's already broken and he doesn't really care.
   It keeps changin' fast, and it don't last for long. *(To 1st Chorus)*

3. He climbed cathedral mountains, he saw silver clouds below.
   He saw everything as far as you can see.
   And they say that he got crazy once and he tried to touch the sun,
   And he lost a friend but kept his memory.

4. Now he walks in quiet solitude the forests and the streams,
   Seeking grace in every step he takes.
   His sight has turned inside himself to try and understand
   The serenity of a clear blue mountain lake.

   *2nd Chorus:*
   And the Colorado Rocky Mountain high,
   I've seen it rainin' fire in the sky.
   You can talk to God and listen to the casual reply.
   Rocky Mountain high. (In Colorado.)
   Rocky Mountain high. (In Colorado.)

5. Now his life is full of wonder but his heart still knows some fear
   Of a simple thing he cannot comprehend.
   Why they try to tear the mountains down to bring in a couple more,
   More people, more scars upon the land.

   *3rd Chorus:*
   And the Colorado Rocky Mountain high,
   I've seen it rainin' fire in the sky.
   I know he'd be a poorer man if he never saw an eagle fly.
   Rocky Mountain high.

   *4th Chorus:*
   It's a Colorado Rocky Mountain high.
   I've seen it rainin' fire in the sky.
   Friends around the campfire and everybody's high.
   Rock Mountain high. (In Colorado.)

# TAKE ME HOME, COUNTRY ROADS

Words and Music by
John Denver, Bill Danoff,
and Taffy Nivert

ma,_____ take_ me home,_____ coun - try roads._

I hear her voice, in the morn -

in' hour she calls____ me. The ra - di - o__ re - minds__ me of my

home far a - way.__ And driv - in' down_ the road__ I get a

# THIRSTY BOOTS

Words and Music by
Eric Andersen

**Intro**
**Moderately slow, in 2**

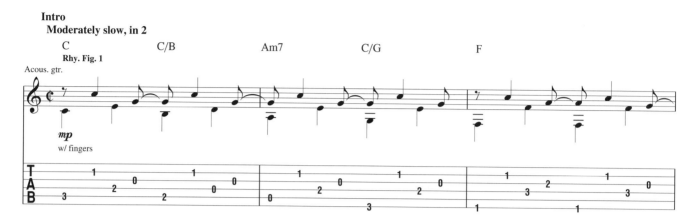

**✶ Verse**

1.You've long _____ been on _____ the o - pen road; _____ you've been sleep-
tell me of _____ the ones you saw _____ as far
_____ you are _____ no stran - ger down _____ the crook

- in' in the rain. _____ From dirt - y words _____ and mud -
_____ as you could see, _____ a - cross the plains _____ from field _____
- ed rain - bow trails, _____ from danc - ing cliff - edged shat -

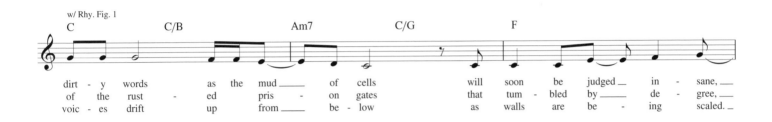

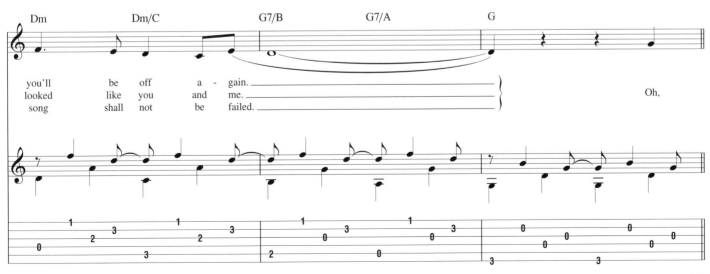

take off ___ your thirst - y boots ___ and stay for a while. ___ Your

feet are hot ___ and wea - ry ___ from a dust - y mile. ___ And

w/ Rhy. Fig. 2

may - be I ___ can make ___ you laugh, ___ and may - be I ___ can try.

___ Just look - in' for ___ the eve - ning

*To Coda* ⊕

w/ Rhy. Fig. 1 (1st 2 meas.)

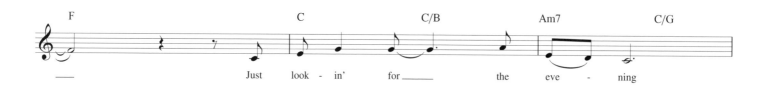

and the morn - in' in your eye. ___

# THIS OLD GUITAR

Words and Music by
John Denver

* Use thumb

* To play along with recording, place capo at 2nd fret.

*Additional Lyrics*

2. This old guitar gave me my lovely lady,
   It opened up her eyes and ears to me.
   It brought us close together, and I guess it broke her heart.
   It opened up the space for us to be.
   What a lovely place and a lovely space to be.

3. This old guitar gave me my life, my living,
   All the things you know I love to do,
   To serenade the stars that shine from a sunny mountainside,
   And most of all to sing my songs for you.
   I love to sing my songs for you, *(etc.)*

# TODAY

Words and Music by
Randy Sparks

*All music sounds a minor 3rd higher than written. Capoed fret is "0" in tab.

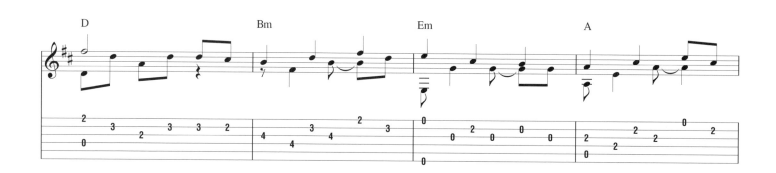

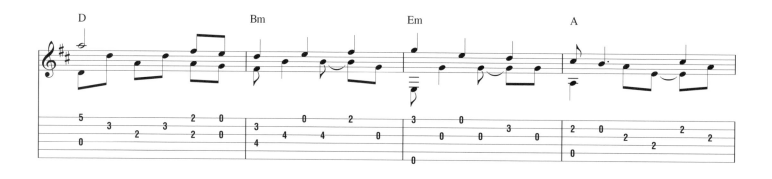

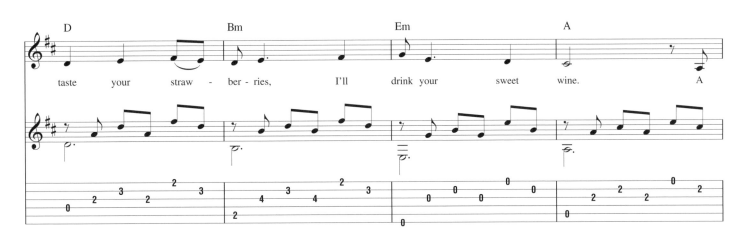

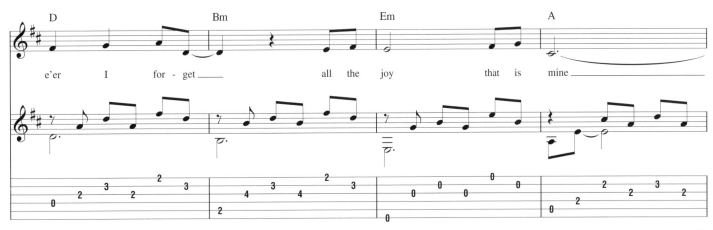

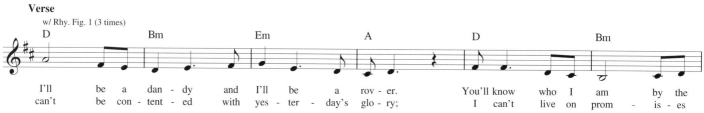

**Verse**

w/ Rhy. Fig. 1 (3 times)

I'll be a dan - dy and I'll be a rov - er. You'll know who I am by the
can't be con - tent - ed with yes - ter - day's glo - ry; I can't live on prom - is - es

songs that I sing. I'll feast at your ta - ble, I'll sleep in your clo - ver.
win - ter to spring. To - day is my mo - ment and now is my sto - ry.

*2nd time, D.S. al Coda*

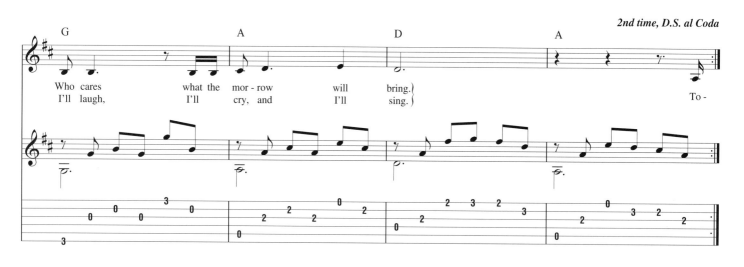

Who cares what the mor - row will bring.
I'll laugh, I'll cry, and I'll sing. To -

**Coda**

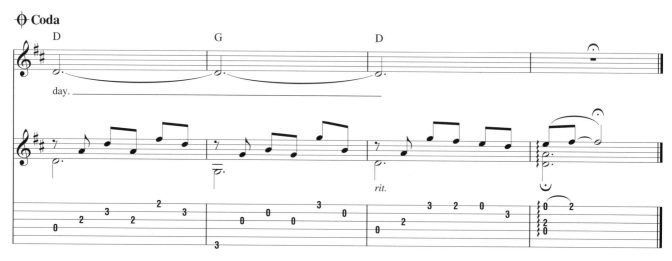

day.

*rit.*

# Cherry Lane Music is your source for
# JOHN DENVER SONGBOOKS!

## PIANO/VOCAL BOOKS

### JOHN DENVER ANTHOLOGY
A collection of 54 of this music legend's greatest tunes, including: Annie's Song • Follow Me • Leaving on a Jet Plane • Rocky Mountain High • Sunshine on My Shoulders • and more, plus a biography and John's reflections on his many memorable songs.
_____02502165 Piano/Vocal/Guitar..........................$22.95

### THE BEST OF JOHN DENVER – EASY PIANO
A collection of 18 Denver classics arranged for easy piano. Contains: Leaving on a Jet Plane • Take Me Home, Country Roads • Rocky Mountain High • Follow Me • and more.
_____02505512 Easy Piano ............................................$9.95

### THE BEST OF JOHN DENVER – PIANO SOLOS
_Best of John Denver – Piano Solos_ is a fabulous collection of 10 greatest hits from the legendary country artist. It includes many of his major hits including: Annie's Song • Leaving on a Jet Plane • Rocky Mountain High • and Take Me Home, Country Roads.
_____02503629 Piano Solo ..........................................$10.95

### JOHN DENVER – A CELEBRATION OF LIFE
The matching folio to the legendary songwriter/performer's album features some of his most popular songs. Includes: Rocky Mountain High • Leaving on a Jet Plane • Whispering Jesse • and more, plus photos and biographical information.
_____02502227 Piano/Vocal/Guitar.............................$14.95

### A JOHN DENVER CHRISTMAS
A delightful collection of Christmas songs and carols recorded by John Denver. Includes traditional carols (Deck the Halls • Hark! The Herald Angels Sing • The Twelve Days of Christmas) as well as such contemporary songs as: A Baby Just Like You • Christmas for Cowboys • Christmas Like a Lullaby • and The Peace Carol.
_____02500002 Piano/Vocal/Guitar.............................$14.95

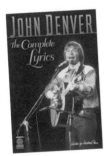

### JOHN DENVER: THE COMPLETE LYRICS
An extremely gifted singer/songwriter, John Denver possessed the unique ability to marry melodic music with gentle, thought-provoking words that endeared him to his countless fans. Now, for the first time ever, John Denver's lyrics have been printed in their entirety: no other book like this exists! It contains lyrics to more than 200 songs, and includes an annotated discography showing all the songs, and an index of first lines. This collection also features an introduction by Tom Paxton, and a foreword from Milt Okun, John Denver's first record producer, and the founder of Cherry Lane Music.
_____02500459 ...........................................................$16.95

### JOHN DENVER'S GREATEST HITS
This collection combines all of the songs from Denver's three best-selling greatest hits albums. 34 songs in all, including: Leaving on a Jet Plane • For Baby (For Bobbie) • Thank God I'm a Country Boy • Annie's Song • Perhaps Love • I Want to Live.
_____02502166 Piano/Vocal/Guitar.............................$17.95

### JOHN DENVER – A LEGACY OF SONG
This collection celebrates one of the world's most popular and prolific entertainers. Features 25 of John's best-loved songs with his commentary on each: Annie's Song • Fly Away • Leaving on a Jet Plane • Rocky Mountain High • Sunshine on My Shoulders • Take Me Home, Country Roads • Thank God I'm a Country Boy • and more, plus a biography, discography, reflections on John's numerous accomplishments, and photos spanning his entire career.
_____02502151 Piano/Vocal/Guitar Softcover.........................$24.95
_____02502152 Piano/Vocal/Guitar Hardcover ......................$34.95

## JOHN DENVER & THE MUPPETS – A CHRISTMAS TOGETHER
Back by popular demand! This book featuring John Denver, Kermit, and all the Muppets includes 12 holiday songs: A Baby Just like You • Carol for a Christmas Tree • Christmas Is Coming • The Christmas Wish • Deck the Halls • Have Yourself a Merry Little Christmas • Little Saint Nick • Noel: Christmas Eve, 1913 • The Peace Carol • Silent Night, Holy Night • The Twelve Days of Christmas • We Wish You a Merry Christmas.
_____02500501 Piano/Vocal/Guitar................................$9.95

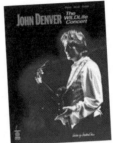

### JOHN DENVER – THE WILDLIFE CONCERT
This matching folio to John Denver's second live album – a two-CD set accompanying a cable TV special and home video – features 29 fabulous tracks: Amazon • Annie's Song • Bet on the Blues • Calypso • Darcy Farrow • Eagles and Horses • Falling Out of Love • The Harder They Fall • Is It Love? • Leaving on a Jet Plane • Me and My Uncle • A Song for All Lovers • Sunshine on My Shoulders • You Say That the Battle Is Over • and more.
_____02500326 Piano/Vocal/Guitar.............................$17.95

## P/V/G SHEET MUSIC

_____02504223 Annie's Song....................................................$3.95
_____02504206 Follow Me........................................................$3.95
_____02504181 For You...........................................................$3.95
_____02504225 Leaving on a Jet Plane.....................................$3.95
_____02509538 Perhaps Love...................................................$3.95
_____02504219 Sunshine on My Shoulders................................$3.95
_____02504214 Take Me Home, Country Roads .........................$3.95
_____02509523 Thank God I'm a Country Boy............................$3.95

## GUITAR BOOKS

### JOHN DENVER ANTHOLOGY FOR EASY GUITAR
This superb collection of 42 great Denver songs made easy for guitar includes: Annie's Song • Leaving on a Jet Plane • Take Me Home, Country Roads • plus performance notes, a biography, and Denver's thoughts on the songs.
_____02506878 Easy Guitar........................................$15.95

### JOHN DENVER AUTHENTIC GUITAR STYLE
12 never-before-published acoustic guitar note-for-note transcriptions of the most popular songs by John Denver. Includes the hits: Annie's Song • Sunshine on My Shoulders • Take Me Home, Country Roads • and more.
_____02506901 Acoustic Guitar Transcriptions.......................$14.95

### THE BEST OF JOHN DENVER
Over 20 of Denver's best-known hits spanning his 25-year career! Includes: Annie's Song • Leaving on a Jet Plane • Rocky Mountain High • Thank God I'm a Country Boy • Sunshine on My Shoulders • and more.
_____02506879 Easy Guitar........................................$9.95

### JOHN DENVER – GREATEST HITS FOR FINGERSTYLE GUITAR
For the first time ever, 11 favorite Denver standards in fingerstyle arrangements that incorporate the melodies of the songs and can thus be played as solo guitar pieces or vocal accompaniments. Includes: Annie's Song • Leaving on a Jet Plane • Rocky Mountain High • and more.
_____02506928 Fingerstyle Guitar..............................................$14.95

_For a complete listing of available Cherry Lane titles, please visit our web site at_ **www.cherrylane.com**

**CHERRY LANE MUSIC COMPANY**
6 East 32nd Street, New York, NY 10016
_Quality in Printed Music_

Exclusively Distributed By
**HAL•LEONARD® CORPORATION**
7777 W. Bluemound Rd. P.O. Box 13819 Milwaukee, WI 53213

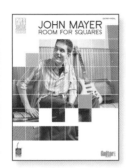

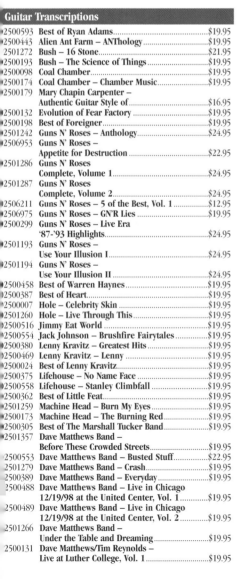